CREEPING THYME

CREEPING THYME

by Ronald Pies

Brandylane Publishers, Inc.
Richmond, Virginia

Copyright © 2004 by Ronald Pies
All rights reserved.
Printed in the United States of America

Brandylane Publishers, Inc.
Richmond, Virginia
804.644.3090
800.553.6922
brandy@crosslink.net
www.brandylanepublishers.com

ISBN 1-883911-58-3

Library of Congress Control Number
2004090444

Cover concept and design by Jeanne Minnix and Tom Trenz

To Nancy, who plants the seeds…

CONTENTS

Spell-check for a Malformed Fetus	1
Old Ladder-Back	2
Creeping Thyme	3
The Salem Elegies	4
Hunting Season, Biddeford, Maine	12
Sitting Shivah	14
Riding Down Dark	16
What's Right	17
White Out	18
Weeds in Winter—*After Lauren Brown*	20
Voices	22
To Dr. Paul Mendelsohn	26
Table Talk	28
Plane Crash	30
Styx	31
Dark and Bright	33
Consultation Request	35
Forearmed	36
Three Patients	37
April's Wood	40
Visitant	41
Reflections	44
Smoke, Lilac, Lemon	45
Crisis—*for D.P.T.*	47
Memento	48
White-Coat Hypertension	49
After Asphodel—*for W.C.W.*	51
My Father's Shadows	52
Persimmon Tree Road—*for D.B.*	53
Voice Mail	56
Fulbourn, Spring 1980	57
Wound in a Rainbow—*for S.D.*	60
Migrations—*for W.D.S.*	64

Night Call	70
St. Maarten's Fire	71
To My Uncle Jack	72
At Cousin Anne's	74
Prolapse of the Uterus	76
Purple Loosestrife	77
Missing Children	78
Grandfather	79
Airport Wheelchair	81
Utah Juniper	83
Congestive Heart Failure	85
The Leonid Meteor Shower, After 9-11	86
The Alzheimer Sonnets	87
Jewish Piano	89
Hard Night—*for Helena*	91
The Neurology Professor Retires	92
Kennebunk Pond *In Memoriam*	93
In Memoriam, Ilan Ramon	94
Squirrels	95

FOREWORD

Ron Pies is a poet-psychiatrist whose steady and sensitive eye and compassionate heart radiate through the poems of *Creeping Thyme*. Using his characteristic spare line, Dr. Pies tells us, "Another Spring / has made us younger / and older" (from "To Dr. Paul Mendolsohn"). Indeed, these poems do the same. They make us younger because of their freshness and energy. They make us older because of their experience and pain. This fine collection of poems tells us of patients and family, of love and loss. In doing so, Ron Pies' work reflects the tension between tenderness and steadiness that lies at the heart of medical practice, and perhaps at the heart of good poetry as well.

Jack Coulehan, MD
Author, *Medicine Stone*

PREFACE

I have a feeling that the less poets say about their poetry, the better. So I will let the late Primo Levi speak to the generative spirit of these poems:

"We are here for this—to make mistakes and to correct ourselves, to stand the blows and hand them out. We must never feel disarmed: nature is immense and complex, but it is not impermeable to the intelligence; we must circle around it, pierce and probe it, look for the opening or make it."

—from *The Periodic Table*

ACKNOWLEDGEMENTS

Some of these poems, or earlier versions of them, appeared in the following publications:
Poetica (Jewish Piano), *The Literary Review* (Voices; Missing Children); *Response* (Sitting Shivah); *Poetpourri* [Comstock Review] (Old Ladder Back; Purple Loosestrife; Martha Cory; Airport Wheelchair); *Voices West* (Reflections); *Midstream* (Hunting Season, Biddeford, Maine); *Connecticut River Review* (Smoke, Lilac, Lemon; Kennebunk Pond: In memorium); *The Healing Muse* (Hard Night; My Father's Shadows); *Mima'amakim* (Ilan Ramon, in Memoriam).

I would also like to thank the *Journal of the American Medical Association* for permission to reprint, in original or modified form, the following poems:

Spell-check for a Malformed Fetus—vol. 273, No. 18 (May 10, 1995)
Styx—vol. 270, No. 18 (Nov. 10, 1993)
Emily—vol. 263, No. 2 (Jan. 12, 1990) p. 316.
Consultation Request—vol. 267, No. 5 (Feb. 5, 1992)
Congestive Heart Failure—vol. 288, No 16 (Oct. 23, 2002) p. 1952
The Alzheimer Sonnets-1-4—in vol 286, Nos. 8 & 9, (Aug. 22/29 and Sept 5, 2001), p. 892 and p. 1013.
The Neurology Professor Retires—vol 283, No. 19 (May 17, 2000) p. 2499.

Thanks also to Margot Wiznansky, for permission to reprint "St. Maarten's Fire" originally published in: *Mercy of Tides: Poems for a Beach House* (anthology edited by Margot Wizansky), Salt Marsh Pottery Press, Dartmouth MA, 2003.

I would also like to acknowledge Carolyn Page and Roy Zarucchi for their work on my last chapbook, *Riding Down Dark* (Nightshade Press, 1992), in which some of these poems appeared.

My appreciation to Robert Pruett, Debra Bruce, W.D. Snodgrass, Steve Pantani, Richard Berlin, Robert Deluty, Manuel Mota, Richard Hart Phillips, Mantosh Dewan, Charlene Breedlove, Elissa Ely, Charles Fishman, Gouri Datta, Sasha Helper and many other friends and colleagues for their encouragement over the years. I also thank my patients for educating me in courage and endurance.

My special appreciation goes to Jack Coulehan MD, for his generous reading of, and comments on, my manuscript.

Finally, thanks, in memoriam, to my father, Jacob Pies; to my mother, Frances Pies Oliver; to my sister, Diane Pies Toby; and my brother, Harvey Pies, for their inspiration and encouragement.

SPELL-CHECK FOR
A MALFORMED FETUS

In my laptop's lexicon,
   there are no words
for your body's chaos—
   each lesion in my write-up
is searched back to normalcy.
   "Mitral" scans
as mistral,
   that cold, sere wind
off southern France;
   "dysmelia"
comes up dismay.

In these quick, cool chips,
   catastrophe is sent
to finishing school:
   "agyria" becomes agile,
"teratosis" goes to tearoom.
Poor remnant:
   if only,
in your first fission,
   some godly processor
had blessed
   your blighted genes;
rewritten
   their scattered base-pairs
in lucid script.

OLD LADDER-BACK

You have worried
   this antique chair
down to its blond bones,
   your hands a blur
of sandpaper dust.
   Too bad the stencils
had to go,
   but you are digging
for the bare heart
   of this laddered frame.
Then, like a face rising
   through stirred water,
we see
   ARNELL 1843
emerge beneath the seat:
   the fashioner
of this lean comfort?
   A plank that says,
Sit in peace, but don't
   slouch.

   As you sand and scrape,
I see old Arnell
   living close
to winter's sockets,
   answering
with strong, shaped wood.

CREEPING THYME

We are out burying bulbs
   in the mock-summer heat
of mid-October.
   Our chart proclaims,
"Nature's Miracles
   from Holland!"
then warns:
   "In cold climates,
plant bulbs
   before the first
hard frost."

There is earthy science
   to this:
Galanthus (the Snowdrop)
   goes five inches down,
the Hyacinth, eight.
   Spanish Bluebell, Dutch Iris,
Late Tulip — each
   has its depth, space,
and flowering height.

You and I, nearly forty,
   also bend
to new science,
   our backs
no longer bowstrings.
   Time creeps crisply
to the first hard frost.

THE SALEM ELEGIES

In the year 1692, Salem, Massachusetts was the site of numerous "witchcraft" trials. At least twenty people were executed, mainly by hanging. Most of the early accusers were adolescent girls; most of the eventual victims were women.

PROLOGUE

Where is the city
   that was full of people?
Where, Rebecca Nurse, hanged
   on Gallows Hill,
cut down and buried
   on the hill?
And Giles Cory,
   tongue pressed
from out his body?
   The trees of summer
are hanging wood;
   our children cry
in the spectral
   neighborhood.

Alice Parker, Martha Cory
   and Wilmett Redd
stand now accused;
   in Andover and Marblehead
a cannibal heat
   drums our brains.
Sundered from God,
   we move
soul by soul apart.

We are as shadows
in the bone orchard
   of the heart.

What shall be said
   in your favor,
daughters of Salem?
   Dirges for the dead city
rust in my mouth.

   Husband and wife
sully house
   with false testament.
At night,
   the cattle scream.
Justice
   has no firmament
but the dreams
   of bitter school girls.
Those whelps
   we dandled and nursed
hurl convulsive phlegm;
   our doctors
find no physic
   to chasten them.
No deference
   is shown the elders.
The constables
   by moonlight
breach our locks,
   paw our women
for demon teats
   and witches marks .

On Gallows Hill,
   our sisters' feet

uproot
   the shallow soil.
Smallpox festers
   and locusts
spoil
   the vernal wheat.
And where is Sarah Good,
   whose husband
betrayed her?
   And where,
Susannah Martin?

MARTHA CORY

My husband,
   I blow
among the voices
   of Gallows Hill;
the bitter women
   who hanged with me
hang like smoke
   above the hill
and wild bayberry.
   We lay two weeks
in Salem Jail,
   so many in a cell
we soaked
   in each other's water.
Then they took me to Boston
   while you had trial.
They dragged you to the field
   beside the courthouse,
pressed you there
   until your tongue furled out.
Three days later,

  they took us in a cart
to Gallows Hill.
  The wheels froze
at the root of the hill,
  and the others prayed.
But I could not still my mind
  for prayer.
There was only that house
  sixty years ago,
and two young people
  mixing rust
and sour milk
  to paint the barn;
the smell of flax
  in the flax break,
the pull
  of tightening yarn.
Those flowers
  on Gallows Hill
smelled much
  like our candles.
Best of men
  and most handsome:
how did we,
  who kept law and Sabbath,
come to this?

GILES CORY

I am the man
  they crushed with rocks
piled on broad beams;
  Giles Cory, a farmer
these sixty years.
  They staked me

to the ground
   so that the ropes
bit my wrists, then pried me
   for confession.
I spoke
   not a blessed
Christian word.
   Old Corwin, the sheriff,
piled rock on rock
   until my ribs cracked
and the air whistled
   from my lungs.
I asked for more weight,
   the better to die quickly.
They told me
   I'd be digging
my own shallow grave
   if I didn't confess.

Well, wife: I thought
   of our barn
that winter
   the snow lay two feet
in the field;
   how the roof groaned
and the frame bent
   but did not break.
You were with child,
   and the locusts
had snatched the grain
   that fall.
We shored the barn back up
   and saw you to term.
Best of women: how did we,
   who did our share in Church,
who spoke proper prayers

and bent our backs in labor—
how did we
   come to this?

THE REVEREND SAMUEL PARRIS

He who hung
   on that rood wood
would brook no clemency;
   no ruth for hags
who fly
   through stinking night
and feel
   no corporal pain:
such are not
   for clemency.
He who rose
   on that third day
will set no foot
   where heresy is loosed,
where harlots spawning imps
   importune clemency.
He who crossed
   from God to Man
forbears no fits
   among our girls,
nor lets the wedge
   of pity
dissever congregation.
   No witch
can merit clemency.
   Each witch and wizard
brings down
   our pristine Christian
fold.

No mercy flows
to banshee, elf, or ghoul
   or to the maggots
of the soul
   or usurious Jew—
such are for the rope
   that swings
and not for clemency.

EPILOGUE

Blood and butchery
   were not always
upon this land.
   I recall
on the cusp of Spring
   the first bird stirrings
and sprouts of cyclamen,
   the bayberry clumps
on the banks
   of spawning streams.
I recall
   husband and wife
in true matrimony,
   in human decency,
breast to breast
   and thigh on thigh
in the thicket
   by Beadle's Tavern,
owls whooing
   in the star-blind night—
and dreams of dancing
   on Salem Green,
men and women spun round
   like fresh cream

and the scent
    of sweet woodruff
on the wind.
    All seemed green,
endless green,
    in this Massachusetts,
our new Eden.
    Daughters of Salem,
we are wholly innocent
    of wickedness.
Let us pray
    for the ruckling of doves
among these nighthawks.

HUNTING SEASON, BIDDEFORD, MAINE

Outside
   BB's Country Store,
we see the rump end
   of a buff-brown deer,
trussed and tucked
   in the back
of a blue Ford pick-up.

To a Jewish boy
   from Poughkeepsie,
this is redneck stuff,
   or worse—
my grandfather's family,
   stalked and felled
in Poland's woods,
   sport
for the Master Race.

No, you say—
   these herds would starve
this December
   without the hunters'
blast of grace.
   Which would you choose:
winter's feral pangs
   in your belly,
or a bullet
   to the heart?

In nature's cruel economy,
   I guess you're right.
But I wonder, still,
   if revelation flickered

in those hunted eyes,
    and whispered,
The world is cold,
    cold—
and God will not save you.

SITTING SHIVAH*

Outside
   our fifth-floor window,
the sumacs swish
   like horses' tails
in mid-June wind.
   You loved the way
this grove
   would swell in summer,
thin
   by late October,
and fatten out
   in May again.
Like phantom pain
   that binds the soldier
to his severed limb,
   your scent
still conjoins us
   in our bed.

This morning
   I thought the wind blew
a chant
   in bastard Hebrew,
your only *kaddish*.
   Covering my ears,
I recalled
   how custom says
to cover mirrors
   for a week,
putting vanity aside.
   But the old,
haunted Jews
   knew the truth:
without a sheet

    upon it,
each mirror
    grins back the teeth
of the dead.

* Shivah, from the Hebrew, "seven": the seven days of mourning for the dead. The mourner's kaddish is a memorial prayer.

RIDING DOWN DARK

You've earned sweet sleep
   tonight, my love:
your note pad brims
   with two hours
of sketched horses,
   born of your patient's
nightmare call:
   she is poised again
between hope
   and whetted steel.
You are here
   to talk her down,
bridle fury,
   ride out rage.
These marginal horses
   you've drawn—
full-rumped, dark-eyed,
   eager for gale—
have just the force
   your patient lacks:
all her seeming storms
   are mostly pain.
The voices she hears
   are not the wind
to stir
   your stallion's mane.

WHAT'S RIGHT

You sit
   with your hands twined
in loose wool
   and knitting needles,
confusing my sense of side.
   If there's a ring
beneath your fabric,
   is it on the left or right?
Is it plain talk
   and coffee for us,
or my lips
   pressing yours
with wine?

Seen from here,
   left is right
and right is left,
   like the heart's
cold X-rays
   that threw me
in school.
   I'm counting fingers
through the quick purling
   of your wool.
Lady, why not bring
   your open hands to me,
and to hell
   with what's right?

WHITE-OUT

Ten years
   bring me back
to Ithaca;
   a receding, snow-blind
older man.
   The students laugh
in a child's tremolo;
   all their sweaters
are Woolite-white.
   Some hormone storm
has swathed my brain
   in snow,
and loosed a child's
   appetite.

In the coffee house
   on Eddy Street,
I watch the flocks
   of frozen breasts,
unattainable hips.
   In six more years,
I'll be a father
   to the freshman:
a wholly-altered
   rack of flesh.
Age must team
   with gravity
to draw us down
   from head to legs,

to draw the hair
   from scalp to face
and leave us all
   a bunch of grinning
neutered pears.

    I have a title,
job, and wife,
    yet drift
to this bleached place
    of lust's cartoons,
where reminiscence
    dazzles sight.

On the drive back,
    past the gutted cattails
and dead shanks
    of corn,
I find myself
    on some unnatural
road.
    I bring the car
round,
    and lurch headlong
through runnels
    of blasted snow,
eddying
    like witch's smoke
upon a stage;
    past the shut-down
chicken franchises,
    the ice-cliffs
hung in walrus tusks,
    the highway maintenance
stations.
    Finally
a piece of sign
    shows through
its caul.
    The ordered letters
of our city
    deliver me
to obligation.

WEEDS IN WINTER
—After Lauren Brown

You can recognize them still:
   old tatters of winter,
spidery fingers, chilled
   against the snow:
foxtail grass, lady's slipper,
   dogbane: they persist
but will not grow:
   wrecks of xylem and phloem,
brittle, changeless, dull.

Here is the cornfield
   of last August's storm.
Old husks, old stalks,
   a variegated ear
no crow could eat,
   the kernels changed
to nubs of stone.
   That day,
the lightening ripped.
   Hail fell, and the corn
was full to catch it.
   You tugged my sleeve
to rush us home.

Old hats, old furs,
   we are back
to vervain and cocklebur
   in the woods
behind your house.
   Back by the spider's rock
and the starving deer,
   the unclaimed feral dogs.
All that grows, or might,

is skulled or mummified,
stony as the child
   in the womb
that died.

If we move quickly,
   I say,
the old life
   might come back.
You point to where a squirrel's
   track
gets scuffled
   in larger prints;
a fox, or wolf, perhaps:
   whatever prays on negligence.

Had I seized you
   five years ago,
would you have spilled
   like milkweed,
Or put up prickles
   to my hand?
"Hawthorn and gentian
   will grow here soon,"
you say.

And these woods
   are still
untrammeled land.

VOICES
—for Elie Wiesel

One hundred men,
   they marched us from Birkenau
to Buno.
   One hundred of us,
they lit our way
   with machine gun,
closed our eyes
   in the closing snow.
Rabbi Eliahu,
   the radiant one,
scratched the snowbanks
   for his son,
pushed the mangled
   from the snows
to clear his son's throat
   of unshod feet
and newspapers
   advertising strudel.
We ran,
   and dreamed of soup.
We ran from the guns,
   from the myriad dead tales
of mercy,
   ran for a wall
to sleep against,
   to fold our idiot shoulders,
ran from our sons
   who fattened
the piling snow.

When they took Hephzibah
to the ovens,
I walked out

*to the edge of camp
so that the sun
could scald my eyes
and the frozen ground
swell
and fold me in
like a gullet.
But the Kapo found me,
lurched my shoulders up,
striking my face.
They were good,
those nubby fingers;
sharp and sweet
pungent as chimneys.*

*I thought of cabbage broth,
the Shabbas,
the lemon and the lemon rind.
Do you recall,
my husband,
how on Shabbas
Hephzibah would wear
that velvet dress,
teaching you to dance?*

I recall
   that they marched us
from Birkenau to Buno.
   One hundred men,
we stopped
   when the Gestapo pissed
or the sirens thickened,
   the Americans
bombing around us,
   that steel
dropping sweeter than manna.

    I recall
that through the sirens
    I heard singing:
my father,
    who knew Talmud and Midrash,
who tore no paper
    on Shabbas,
who washed his hands
    before wrapping tefilin.
For me, a boy of nine,
    it was a worship of smells:
grape wine brimmed in a goblet,
    damp books lining
the cedar shelves.
    Father,
in my nostrils
    there is only the human bread
of Birkenau.

Before they shaved our heads,
I would think back
to the parties in Krakow;
to a boy
neither husband
nor lover,
before the signs went up,
before they searched us
for prayer books,
when there was breeze
and garden
and rowing in the park.

My husband,
they have stopped
giving out potatoes
here.

The ink on my wrist
is heavy.
Do you remember
the balloons
with chocolate inside?

I remember
   that on the train
to Buchenwald,
   a son
clawed his father
   for a crust of bread.
A father lay singing
   in a pool of urine,
and the living lay
   in the trousers
of the dead.
   When we stopped at Breslau,
the workers
   threw rolls at us;
through the slats,
   we watched businessmen
in long furs,
   sleek ladies
in German hats.
   Rabbi Eliahu
was still singing
   in the corner:
"If there is a God,
   if there is,
he should be strangled
   slowly."

TO DR. PAUL MENDELSOHN

*My Former Student,
Killed while Jogging*

Paul,
   I didn't know you well,
but still recall
   your almost famous name,
your European face,
   honed as fingers
across an old-world keyboard.
   Had you died in a duel
on some grassy slope
   near Leipzig,
I might have bought it—
   but this jogging stuff
on a sunny Saturday
   was no way to go
(not that guns
   or other mortal exits
show much grace).

Racing
   into the sun,
mowed down from behind,
   you gave
(a witness said)
   one melting glance
across your shoulder.
   Today, Boston
has its marathon.
   Another Spring
has made us younger
   and older.
And you,

  like Bruegel's Icarus,
fell tumbling
  from your life
while runners knelt
  to lace their shoes.

TABLE TALK

   In the kitchen
of our summer house,
   the table talk
never changes:
   who is single,
who is fat;
   who has fallen
into cancer, arthritis,
   or debt.

Prosperous cousins
   have stopped coming;
we get cards
   from Spanish-sounding
places.
   Yet the gone
and dead
   filter in
with coffee smells,
   lox, and cake.
They fill our mouths
   like raisins
we wish were sweeter.

   The rolls are buttered
and buttered.
   Baby pictures
flap
   in our wallets
like the wings
   of ardent moths,
bellied out
   in the dish
of our outdoor
   light.

All these years,
we have been feeding
against the flame.

PLANE CRASH

I don't know why I fear
   that sudden mesh
of bone and steel;
   or dream
how blighted metal
   flies
phosphorescent
   down the rim of sky,

   scattering me
with aluminum foil
   over someone's
shaded suburb.

Calculation proves
   the chances small
for sudden bolt
   on wing;
but in the plexiglass
   window,
I see the grin
   that cancels
everything.

STYX

Crazy
   as the Devil's
bedbugs,
   reviler of Jews,
would-be assassin
   of kings:
you came in
   "q. 3 months"
for feeble doses
   of Thorazine,
the limit fixed
   by your mystic
numerology.

You changed your name
   to "Styx,"
the dark-most river
   of Hell,
and had it blazoned
   on your Medicaid card.

Three years
   you pressed your case
with me-
   how the Dean
had passed you over
   for department chair-
Another Semitic conspiracy!-
   despite your scheme
to transmute coal gas
   into gold.

You sent me letters
   signed,

"Styx and Stones
   will break your bones,"
and swatted down
   my words
like bubonic fleas.

When I told you
   I'd be leaving soon,
you grew ungodly still;
   then, with the shudder
of some creature
   about to molt, said,
"I'm quite horribly ill,
   aren't I?"
and grabbed your coat.

Where
   in my "mental status"
do I note
   how your dark flower
opened
   one frail moment,
then deftly closed?

DARK AND BRIGHT

Mrs. Thomas,
   my fingers curl
in your floury palm.
   You look at me
through cataracts
   and retinal bleeds;
You, who mothered
   forty broods
of jejune girls
   through Bronte and Keats,
and ended up unsightly,
   living with your daughter.
One morning,
   she slapped the oatmeal down,
and you knew
   to take your leave.

But the nurses
   aren't much better.
You squirreled their pills
   in the pouch
of your cheek,
   and almost dried away.
Perhaps the soup
   is poisoned.
Perhaps—who knows?—
   those nurses on TV
who killed their patient...

But you are safe here.
   The surgeons say
they'll pace your heart
   back to grace.
And you are well fed.

  Keats had a certain charm;
but Byron—he
  was your old true darling.

Two big tumors
  grew from your bowel
last spring;
  now your breast blooms
in kindred buds.
  Upper plates, lowers;
teeth followed eyes
  in the slow fall
that all the body knows.

  You play your tapes
of Dickens
  and see bright shadows pass.
The nurse
  will tuck the sheet
about your toes.

CONSULTATION REQUEST

In my office today,
   I saw a girl
with lightless eyes.
   I checked my books
to learn
   what might go wrong
with cornea, iris, lens—
   how the light
through a child's eye
   should filter and bend.
Not much came of this,
   or calls to ophthalmologists.
I did discover
   the girl was beaten
some
   by her father and mother.

Did I not get
   my optics right?
Or does the soul's prism,
   once kicked out of kilter,
no longer
   refract the light?

FOREARMED

The Jewish ladies
   in McDonald's
in Brookline
   wear heavy coats
in summer,
   clutched
against
   who knows what
demented snows
   or recurrent
German death.

THREE PATIENTS

1.
Emily,
   the snows are settling
on the thickened earth.
   Old black women
break bitter hips
   on Marshall Street.
Your lungs
   grow pregnant again
with their thick birth.

Of winter's legion children,
   I cannot say
why you were maimed;
   your tangled gene
tells only process
   in its tight folds,
and claims no justice
   in your pain.

Again this morning,
   we play our special
winter game;
   backslaps, face mask,
a pot
   to catch your phlegm;
we call your mist tent
   an igloo,
we call you
   my Eskimo wife.
In your watery den
   I tell you stories
about wolves.
   You write my name

on steamed plastic.

2.
Regina,
in a year or more,
   or ten,
you will be lost to me,
   your brown skin
sprouting fistula,
   your war with ulcer
and ileostomy
   slowly at an end.

You smile
   when I bring books
on Magritte;
   we talk
of canvass and oil,
   your studio
off 19th Street.
   On morning rounds,
I see your brush flash
   in the antiseptic sun:
paint is put
   to canvas;
your craft persists.
   Again today,
the blood tests
   must be done.

3.
Mr. Flynn,
   you watch them
wheel your wife
   to the O.R.
I judge

    from your gold suspenders,
your bow tie
    decked with soldiers,
I judge
    from your full eye
that you have had
    a good life together.
Perhaps your passion
    was the sip
of fresh coffee
    those Sunday mornings
when Ed and Elsie called
    and the game
was on channel three.
    Or else you grew tomatoes
and your wife
    chastised you
for the dirt
    in your trouser cuffs.
Perhaps you scoffed
    when she showed you
the lump,
    the dull dimpling
of skin.
    You wear
your soldiers well,
    Mr. Flynn.

APRIL'S WOOD

In our April yard,
   you're splitting logs
for next December,
   knowing green wood
must season and dry.
   The larger world,
like winter,
   may be harder,
colder;
   but every thump
that brings
   your sledgehammer down,
each arc of your shoulder
   reclaims our land
and season's order.
   Smiling, you hold
a wedge of wood
   above your head
like a pioneer's trophy.

VISITANT

I've flown down
   this weekend
to your unwintered
   spring
and fish-net hammock
   in your yard.
The older
   and surer
of us two boys,
   You've done well
in the staid
   Floridian sun.
I've come from Boston,
   just visiting
your life,
   buried
with tales of snow.

   I've watched your son,
my nephew,
   grow
from yelping bundle
   to the reigning
prodigy
   of your house.
At two,
   he knew my name;
at three,
   he christened me
uncle.
   All that ride
from Jacksonville,
   you played the tape
of his favorite

  song:
the owl
 and the pussycat
went to sea
 in a beautiful
pea-green boat.
  I feared
so mortally
  for his gurgling
life,
  I double-locked
the belt
  about his seat.

Here
  in your Planned Community
you've settled in
  to sparser hair,
tennis courts
  and gate.
Nothing could bleed
  amidst these tricycles
and outdoor grills,
  though many things
will die:
  your neighbor's cat
neatly killed
  beneath
the push-button
  garage door.

Still,
you've overcome
  the fated heart
in me
  that knows

all good
   will fall apart.
Odder
   with each single
year,
   I've come again,
just visiting
   your life:
the house
   I wouldn't make,
the child and wife.
   I've pared things down
to a lover
   now and then,
and bare lines
   scraped on paper
crisp as snow.

REFLECTIONS

Thirty years
   you've lain frozen,
my father—
   poised in the spill
of December's lean soil.
   You rise up now,
still smelling
   of catchers' mitts
and spent cigars.
   You bring back summers
in Kibbie Park,
   the bleachers,
back slaps
   and games I wouldn't play.
You're still singing
   "C'est mag-nif-ee-kay"
in the car.

Thirty years
   have slaked the fires
of my shame.
   Yet at night
I see you still
   in your stained
white shirt,
   soaked around the pits,
and hear
   your slow refrain:
"Go out to the park
   and hit a few?"
Even then,
   the bones were showing
through your eyes.

SMOKE, LILAC, LEMON*

Smoke, lilac, lemon—
   if you remember anything
you remember this:
   that smoky kiss,
the night he got back
   from Germany,
hungry for cigarettes,
   sex, and poker;
your lilac talcum
   wrestling the scent
of his Chesterfields,
   the bitter lemon
of his aftershave.
   If you remember anything,
anything
   to stave off
this loosestrife
   of tangle and placque,
it's smoke, lilac
   and lemon,
that jumbalaya place
   just outside New Orleans,
his hands
   inside your skirt.

Smoke, lilac, and—
   Oh, you may not
smell them now,
   but their sweet, sharp
ghosts
   lodge in your heart
like an ax blade
   in a bayou cypress.

A recent study by G. Solomon et al (1998) found that olfactory dysfunction could discriminate between depressed patients and those with Alzheimer's Disease. The "test substances" used included smoke, lilac, and lemon.

CRISIS
—*for D.P.T.*

I've set aside
   my prescription pad
and analytic calm—
   dropped all pretense
of science:
   it's you and me now,
pressed cold
   against death's ribs.
I use
   what tricks I know
to keep you living
   through another bony night,
another flurry
   of final phone calls.
And you, as always, refuting life:
   denaturing love, companions, sex.
Well, you leave my office alive.
   That's as close
to certainty
   as our work gets.

MEMENTO

So you talk to me
   about Brooklyn,
the Jewish Federation dances,
   and how you kept
your cousin Sadie
   from jumping
in front of trains.
   Why bring this up now,
in Boston,
   fifty years
after the facts?

You sit at my table
   with your travel case
of vitamins,
   telling how your mother
kept you out of art school.
   She bought you a stenotype
on the theory
   you'd meet lawyers.
But why tell this
   to your son,
fifty years
   after the facts?

You finger and finger
   the many-colored tablets
of health.
   Your eyes, so blue
they startled men
   into love,
turn briefly
   to sea water.

WHITE-COAT HYPERTENSION*

So many doctors,
so many cool, smiling eyes.
Forty years ago,
I lay in bed, lobster-faced,
and sweated out my heart
for him: the young Dr. Summers.
All he said was, "Scarlatina."
I though he'd scolded me
with a nickname.

Then the boys came:
two terms of pressure cuffs
and magnesium,
my blood so high
it sang in my ears.
Dr. Pressler said,
"Just a little ringing, dear."

At forty,
I found the lump myself.
Dr. McNulty said,
"Mary, that breast
has to go."
I still feel
the way his finger scraped
across the skin
that looked like orange peel.

You saunter in,
and beam down to me
your starched "Good morning."
You cuff me, pump me,
and stroke your chin
in wonder

at my shouting blood

*It has been observed that the patient's blood pressure often rises when the doctor enters the room

AFTER ASPHODEL
—for W.C.W.

In snowless
   late December,
you tug me
   through the yard
to see how life
   persists:
hardy cyclomen, Russian sage,
   and whisps
of sweet woodruff
   have kept
their growing edge.
   Yellow dead-nettle
is anything but dead,
   and even columbine
has lingered.

So why this view
   of death-bed winter,
when there is you—
   elfin as early spring—
to bless
   the green pulse
of our land?

MY FATHER'S SHADOWS

Dead now thirty years,
   Father,
you come back
   as shifting swaths
of white and black,
   ghosts of kidney
probed by sound.
   All this, to track
a single drop
   of pinkish urine.
By the time
   they found your cancer,
you'd been hollowed
   like a cored apple.
But it's my kidneys now,
   And I tell the doctor
I've never felt better.
   "Still," he answers, "still."
Your shadow nudges me
   to ultrasound,
wraps itself
   around my ureters, tubules, veins.
The probe rolls
   through cold gel
spread across my belly,
   each push burbling up
a new image on the screen.
   I watch the technician's eyes
for some kind of verdict.
   "That's a healthy-looking bean,"
she says,
   and the radiologist agrees.
This time, father,
   you shadow me in peace.

PERSIMMON TREE ROAD
—for D.B.

On Persimmon Tree Road
   the hoarded leaves
are burning;
   cords of wood,
dried and stowed
   by provident husbands
are turning
   on the irons.
I've stayed six months
   in this life
I couldn't give you,
   and still don't know
our minds.
   Yesterday morning
you called to say
   you haven't written much—
but there is much
   to revise.
The elms in Iowa city
   are drying;
old friends
   turn mothering wives.
Since you left, you say,
   your poems
have grown gracelessly old.
   In a dream,
you turn me over
   beneath you;
your lover shudders
   to retrieve you.
And I am still living
   on Persimmon Tree Road.

In Autumn
   the chiseled air
brings branch to fragrance
   and leaf
to mulching ground.
   Changeless
in its cadence,
   the season dries
and scuttles round us,
   blows dead summer
in our eyes.
   We jig
through leaf piles
   clasping hands
like ecstatic men
   in umbilical dance.

On Persimmon Tree Road
   the winter bread
is baking.
   Stolid husbands, mindful
how it snowed
   all night, and froze,
are breaking ice
   off the buried walks.
Christmas comes round again.
   We argue greetings
long distance.
   It's costly, these days,
just to talk.
   You say you've mulled over
these seven years
   between us:
the house we never made
   and the vows.
Stubbornness, at least,

    redeems us:
we chew our faults
    then gag them up again
like sodden cows.
    Again this winter,
your apartment's bony cold—
    my lawyer
sends your landlord
    a letter.
You wait out
    our clotted weather
then visit me
    on Persimmon Tree Road.
In summer,
    the fine hard wood
shows white flower
    and fruit
not unlike plum.
    Constant
in its seasons
    persimmon thrives,
circles round us,
    plays its berries
in our thighs.
    There is sweet resolution
in children
    and ripened fruit:
children have your face—
    but the berry
in its season
    gives lovely taste.
And if you count
    the summers
men have shuddered
    with their women,
you still come up persimmon.

VOICE MAIL

In my office,
   your fists
are two shades short
   of death's knuckles:
you bring me lists
   of antidepressants,
hormones, herbs—
   nothing has worked
for you, nothing disturbs
   the tightness
of your pall.
   Yet when I call you
at home,
   your message chirps,
Hi, sorry we can't chat with you.
   We're probably in the pool,
or out barbecuing on the deck...
   In the background, I hear
a daughter's giggles.
   Your outgoing message
is your wildest dream,
   your angel poem.

If I lose you
   and have to phone—
how shall I endure
   such pure laughter?

FULBOURN, SPRING 1980 *

April, and a freakish snow
   on Fulbourn.
Another week
   might bring crocus up
to pry the shards
   of bricks,
or daisy
   to white the fields
out by the new annex.
   But snows have come,
and chilled
   the blond Stelazine lady,
gone to tea
   across the field.
She longs for winds
   to lift her dress
and make her thick
   and moist;
for sunlight
   to kiss the arms
locked in chemical poise.

For twenty pence
   you take the 110 bus
from Fulbourn
   to the college greens.
Those gargoyles
   hissing from the chapel
at Kings
   have held our gothic fears
and fierce imaginings;
   swallowed them in stone
six hundred years.
Thus, the mincing

    meat-faced squires
are spared
    demonic awe;
and the Stelazine lady
    flicks her tongue
in lust
    against the wall.

Mainly it is staring
    over tea
at Fulbourn
    and swallowing
the pill of fashion;
    waiting for clean linen,
tearing paper cups,
    breaking in the new ones
with their revelatory passions.

I knew a man
    at Fulbourn,
bearded in my color
    and of my age
whose eyes I took
    for run-away trains.
I could not look at him
    without my bowel curdling
or wondering
    of our discrepant brains:
how distanced, for how long;
    and what logic
culls the fragment
    from the song?
For the mad spring up
    in sundering
of man from man,
    in dumb hermetic silence

on queue
> at the taxi stand.

Coats off,
> scarves
and all raiments
> of an old chill:
finally, lady,
> April binds us
in her nude weather.
> And you and I
may find some peace
> in this stony place;
take lemon tea
> on Kings Parade
and dine
> with human face.
For we have seen
> what throes
our climate suffers
> and endures.
These years
> I've cared for you
are deeper
> than all snows

A mental institution near Cambridge, England.

WOUND IN A RAINBOW
—for S.D.

I. Wheat-skinned child
   of farmers,
three years ago
   you drove a U-Haul
out from Topeka
   through mid-winter snow,
nearly brakeless,
   without defroster
or radio,
   and set your life
down here.

When we count
   the fruitless cratings
and uncratings since-
   the numberless,
dumb unboxings
   of our lives-
we start to wonder
   what lemming-love
turns men
   to husbands,
or women gladly
   into wives.

When my eyes
   catch your blue
mid-West gaze,
   there's no more meeting
now
   than in wind
across the Kansas plains.

II. Until late January,
   a snowless winter,
crusted dry
   like an old
laceration,
   littered with bulletins
of shut-down steel mills
   and lines
for free cheese.
   Christmas
happened elsewhere:
   on the news at six,
or on the tin-songed
   intercoms
at bankrupt Woolworths.
   Our wire spruce
stayed fixed
   in last year's box.

Sardonic February came:
   great heaps
of Heidi-flakes,
   glutinous
and soaking,
   snarling cars
into stolid chains
   of honking steel.

Like some venerable
   department store
about to fold,
   we inventoried
all the nuptial
   cold specifics:
planned
   who'll get the microwave,

video discs
   and teflon pans.

III. April
   brought manic snows,
wrenched
   from some Thulian
reservoir
   of cold and pain;
brought back
   what we'd planned
to put behind us,
   and explained
to inquisitor friends.

All that spring
   we read of fires, floods
and spasms
   of the crust.
May choked
   our late-shooting
tulips
   with plundering rain.
In Texas,
   twisters plucked
whole houses
   from their roots.
Beneath our skin,
   something sucked at us
like the low,
   killing vortex
keening in.

IV. Finally,
   our looks
look strange to us:

    glazed and painless
as the morphinated
    death
of kind old men.
    When I come
for my mail,
    I see
the lean-penned envelopes
    from Kansas,
and know
    you'll soon go back.
And I have someone
    I'm seeing now,
just north of Nyack.

Strange
    how now and then,
some gyring humor
    twists us round
each other,
    raw as a wound
 in a rainbow.

MIGRATIONS
—for W.D.S.

In the coronary unit,
   the EKG's sing
like wire sparrows.
   Quinidine, lidocaine-
we have balms
   for the bucking heart;
we give digitalis
   to make the wave forms narrow.
Here
   is all manner
of quick elixir;
   here, the sudden spark
that starts old chests
   heaving.
In Boston,
   I put an ear
to your breast
   and timed your breathing:
the nightmare was wrong,
   and you would live.
When this alarm goes off,
   someone's heart
has stuttered,
   and I have remedy
to give.

Who can replace you?
   Your tongue hunts out
the subtlest scents.
   Your curves
grace all verandas.
   Young birds, and I,
eat gladly

    from your hands.
In the morning,
    the sun is baffled
at your brightness
    (if teeth alone
could light a room,
    you would surely
be a nimbus).

    A valley of smells
grows fertile
    between your hair
and skin.
    Your nostrils
whistle out
    the softest wind.

In Bruegel's winter,
    the hunters
must go home
    to beefy hands
and cabbage soup;
    such is Flanders,
rich with children.
    And if you draw a line
from crow to crow,
    you make a parallel
with the ridge
    of sloping snow:
such is order
    in the artist's season.
This winter,
    the Charles froze low
in its bosom.
    You left for Iowa,
her branches starved with ice,

and gave no reason.
In an old painting,
   I am trudging home
to you,
   laden with venison
and quail.

Delectable,
   indispensable,
faithless creatures:
   you shed your oaths
like feathers.
   In Rouen,
we heard parrots
   squawk
in the courtyard.
   We said we'd grow
as mortared
   in our love
as those old
   cathedral stones—
remember how good
   the *frites* were?
We said. We said.
   This pathologic winter
has stopped the rivers
   in their beds.
Icebreakers
   rend
the sclerosed St. Lawrence.
   The silos
have gone tinny.
   And you and I
have packed our hearts
   in salt and rime;
we take the ice to heart

   as anodyne.

Two days respite
   from the snow
and a few
   bright tinglings
of spring.
   The warped roofs
of battered shingles
   and leaden drains
go liquid now.
   Cigarette butts
buried since October
   overrun
the sidewalks.
   I wear my corduroy jacket
again,
   and memory
has melted up enough
   to let me think
of you.
   There is no green
in the dearth of you,
   or storm of birds
breeding
   throat to throat
in lilac.
   Surely
you could color this earth
   with an old voice
before the snows.

Spring now nearly routing
   bronchitic winter:
in the elevators
   at the V.A.,

old troopers,
   tuberculous with memory,
recount the victory
   at Cantigny.
Mold blights
   the pin-striped pajamas.
The first green squads
   are massing
on the trees.

Monday night
   you page me from Iowa,
telling of your slow change.
   Like a mutant spore,
you have blossomed out
   in alien folds;
all those weeks
   of deranged winter
you would not call,
   your icy flower
grappled
   to take hold.

You say the birds
   are flocking again
to your feeder:
   tanager, thrush, and jay,
they do their dance
   for you, they brush
their fattened bellies
   nearer.
In five years,
   I have come to know
your feathered ways:
   the soundless flights,
those throaty percolations,

    that preening show of grace.

Had you died
    or turned a leper,
I might have made
    a case for grief.
But you persist
    unclassified,
a wraithful woman
    of the land;
your vagrance
    breeds no rival
for bitter reprimand.

Heading north,
    the unflagging geese
trace one last migration
    between us.
Mornings, you put hemp
    and millet
outside your window.
I send you charts
    on species and genus.

NIGHT CALL

Two nights
   the geese sang
in a dead blue drone.
   Two skies
bent blackness
   in their throats
distant as dark milk,
   the geese who clacked
like brittle women.
   They called me
to kiss them
   against the moon,
they drew me
   to the wet window
with voices
   sharp as oak.
The geese
   scraped winds
with the song
   of widows.

ST. MAARTEN'S FIRE

In a green-blue nest
   of shoal and sea,
tucked away
   from Caribbean gale
and roiling wave,
   we snorkeled past
some fire coral,
   battering
with our flippers
   their millennial home.
With the first
   needle-burn buzz,
we thought
   we'd cut our arms
on crusted rock—
   but the blaze
drawn down our nerves
   was coral's sting:
silent, communal,
   in the end, benign—
the grave signature
   of who rules this place.

TO MY UNCLE JACK
(whom we all called "Jackie")

How passing strange
   that on Johnny Carson's
last night—
   on the night
before the big
   Memorial Day weekend,
when lilacs
   in our yard
ached with scent—
   how strange
just then
   they'd find your car
out by Sheepshead Bay,
   out
where you'd made
   your end.

I see you still
   in your black chinos
and Brando tee-shirt,
   back when your namesake
strode the White House
   and the nation
had it all:
   women, muscles, guns.
I see you leaning
   in thick July
against our white
   1962 Bonneville,
cracking wise
   with the cousins:
insolent, playful,
   cock-of-the-yard.

What a turn we've done:
   a nation slumped
over the steering wheel—
   and you
and Johnny
   and May's first lilacs
opening their buds
   like veins.

AT COUSIN ANN'S

Labor Day weekend
   brings us together
again:
   an army of aunts,
uncles, and unheard of
   cousins,
penned
   inside your house.
Beneath
   your mixing bowl,
a pamphlet reads,
   "Separation
and Divorce
   in New Jersey."

On the one TV
   he left you,
we show videos
   of ourselves,
mugging
   for the hungry
camera.
   Another brood of us
is caught
   in the high-tech
whirr
   of silicon.

In the hallway
   are photos
of your students,
   pink-laced
and tip-toed,
   grinning

their pirouettes.
   Somewhere
between rehearsals
   your dance
has gone awry,
   changed
to cold chorea.

In your bedroom,
   we patch the family
back together
   on clean cassettes.

PROLAPSE OF THE UTERUS

A farmer's wife, 42 years old, presents in the emergency room with a "bearing down" sensation in her womb. The patient has had two miscarriages, and now notes irregular menses.

I started to learn their names:
    orchis, aquilegia, gentian.
After Billy died—I mean,
    came out wrong—
I lived for those flowers.
    Then Horace,
he got the cord
    wrapped round
his neck,
    and came out blue.
Orchis, aquilegia—
    Reverend Potter, he said
maybe it was comeuppance
    for playin' around,
but I can't think
    what kind of God
would take two babies
    from their momma.
Then this thing starts,
    like Horace coming down,
only limper.
    All I asked
was to grow things.
    Gentian is blue,
you know.
    I can see it blazing
on the lawn.

PURPLE LOOSESTRIFE

You see us
   in quick bursts of purple
along the highway,
   bullying the other flowers;
but you do not know us.
   Sempiternal
on these greening hills,
   we are the shades
of your husbands, fathers,
   sons—
now receptacles
   for idiot bees.
No—this is not myth
   or image, not Daphne
turned to laurel:
   we are where
your men have gone,
   where loose strife
is distraction from grief,
   from lack of lover
or wife.
   Through our pain,
we rage and multiply,
   beating down
the thought of you
   alone
in ravened winter
   or ruckling spring.
In this petaled limbo,
   each man is left
to shout,
   "I am still King,
King of the Flowers!"

MISSING CHILDREN

Kevin Jay
   and John David,
you smile
   in blue dots
from my milk carton,
   your images plucked
from birthday shots,
   heights and weights
listed like nutrients.
   In Sugar Bush
and Des Moines,
   you are ghostly
celebrities,
   poised
by a million
   coffee cups.
Morning mothers,
   their blood
white as milk,
   drink you
back inside.

GRANDFATHER

When you were twenty,
   you sold the backs of chairs:
an immigrant, a Jew,
   they would have traded you
for cattle.
   I am told you taught Hebrew
to the sons of Jacob Lev,
   who laughed
behind your back.
   You fed them bread
dipped in honey.

Last November
   we visited you,
a vestige in terry-cloth,
   hair turned
to winter wheat.
   Your daughter
winged round you
   like a starched butterfly:
cleaning the gums,
   loosening the truss,
salving the desert lips.

Today, your city praises you
   in print.
The sons
   of the sons of Lev
hear beneath their window
   your slow cortege,
and are told
   that a patriarch
has died.
   Minked women

weep for you.
   The earth is hollowed
in your honor.

AIRPORT WHEELCHAIR

You stand
outside the Delta terminal
as the Sky-Cap heads toward you,
wheeling the damn thing—
just a movable frame
of metal and leather,
but your jaw is set
as if the Cossacks
were about to attack—
as if a push in that chair
were a shove into Hell.

Every cell and sinew
rebels against it:
this steely theft
of muscle and bone,
this slap
at eighty years
of raising us kids,
making a home,
getting your degree—
and not a day spent
in the clutches of doctors.

The Sky-Cap smiles
and murmurs consolation.
You look down at the chair
as if it bristled
with high voltage.
At last you sit,
curling your lip
in disgust.
You look up at the Sky-Cap
and say:

"It's just the jewelry, you know. With you around, the crooks won't grab it."

UTAH JUNIPER

We hiked today
   through Utah's canyons,
deaf to all
   but scurrying squirrels
and the crunch
   of desert soil.
Startled
   by the tortured trunk
of a Utah Juniper,
   we stopped to touch
the stiff, grey fibers—
   splayed, as if
by some blast
   within.

Yet out
   of the dun wood
sprang green leaf
   and stone-hard berry,
where death
   and life
in the brooding tree
   had married.

We learned
   how the juniper
chokes off water
   to its own branches,
and so survives
   the desert drought.
The tree's core thrives;
   The inessential limbs
die out.

And you and I
   these thirty years
might have nourished
   a hundred loves,
a hundred lives-
   who knows
what stony fruit
   would have flourished?
Instead,
   we take our chances
with water
   spread
to love's essential
   branches.

CONGESTIVE HEART FAILURE

As deaths go, it's better
   than most-
the self slipping off
   in a sea
of morphined tranquility.
   But for you, grandmother,
who braved Ukrainian
   pogroms,
who read us "*Do not go gentle...*"
   instead of nursery rhymes-
is this the good night
   you choose?

A porcine valve
   might save you,
but you just whistle
   through your teeth.
"Pig gristle in my heart?
   Pffft!"
Look, I argue,
   even God
wouldn't push kosher
   that far.
"Darling," you say,
   "*this* time
I fight the Cossacks
   on my own soil."

* *In the period of 1918-20, Ukrainian soldiers called Haidamacks-descendants of the Cossacks-massacred scores of Jews.*

THE LEONID METEOR SHOWER, AFTER 9-11

Flat on our backs
   in down parkas,
we see
   in the chill black
of November's sky
   not the fatal fall
of September's planes,
   but three thousand sparks
of dusty divinity,
   freed from Leo's
starry mouth.
   Against the void
of shimmering night,
   they shout,
"*More life, more love,
   more light!*"

THE ALZHEIMER SONNETS

1. Apple blossoms and a robin's egg sky
as I climbed higher, dizzying me,
until a fleck of bark fell in my eye.
I remember clear and sharp how that tree
shook my arms off its bearish trunk,
and sent me spinning in free fall,
clawing the air before the final clump
my leaden body made. I crawled
across the yard in league with death,
though my child's mind didn't know it.
I choked back tears and caught my breath,
biting down the pain. I wouldn't show it
then, or now, as the words spin
from my tangled brain—if ever they were in.

2. The barn swallows swooped low
as we made a sweaty clamor in the hay.
Our first lusting tumbled slow
and musky, morning to noon that day.
That was just before our wedding vows
and that first, unbidden birth.
If I could harvest consonants and vowels
the way I ploughed your riven earth
our first nude morning, I'd be pleased.
The doctors say I'm losing parts of me
with each plaque and tangle of disease,
but I won't feel it. I stay lanky and free
in your hay-kissed arms, where fifty years
pass in an eye-blink that knows no tears.

3. Some nights still, I hear the horses cry
and smell the fire scorch their manes.
Death leapt up in our stallion's eye
as I tugged and wrangled with his reins.

You did your best to keep the water
coming, hose down the house,
and get our son and daughter
safe away. I ran to douse
the sparks that harried our lawn,
until, at last, the wailing engines came.
These days, my smell is nearly gone
for fruits and flowers-but old flames
still come back. With luck, I'll catch the
scent that love's blaze makes permanent.

4. The doctors say some pinkish sludge
is what does you in. Gobs of amyloid
and twisted strands that just won't budge
from the brain. Pretty soon, a void
of neurons hangs like some old
moth-eaten sweater, where once
a solid weave of bold
thought reigned. Yet the soul hunts
for clues among the mind's gray runes,
and now and then finds some Rosetta
Stone of memory-an old Sinatra tune
that brings back spirit, if not the letter.
Love, these cells that wink out one by one
are not the song of all that we've become.

JEWISH PIANO

In the hardware store,
   my wife and I
pick out deck stain
   as the clerk chats
with customers,
   his face grandfatherly
behind gold-rimmed glasses.
   Suddenly, his words
are hammer-blows
   between my eyes:
"Yep," he says,
   tapping the cash register,
"Been playin' the Jewish piano
   all day long."

In an eyeblink,
   I am eight again,
riding the schoolbus
   that picks up kids
at St. Joe's.
   A girl in parochial blue
says to me,
   "Jews have cloven hooves,
you know."

In my brain,
   two Talmudic maxims
war:
   "When insulted, refrain
from insulting";
   and:
"Thou shalt surely rebuke
   thy neighbor."
I close the door

   behind me,
and slink out
     into the accusing sun.

HARD NIGHT
—for Helena

True-the way of flesh
   is a down-swept road,
as scripture and physician
   preach.
But we rise up
   on steps of soul,
a ladder
   no racking night
can breach.
   Luther
in his holy gloom
   knew this,
And Buddha by his tree:
   how death
is trumped
   by love and memory.

In the end,
   Spirit holds
the stronger hand—
   and is the bridge
from here
   to that undiscovered
land.

THE NEUROLOGY PROFESSOR RETIRES

Died Without Issue.
   Decessit sine prole,
if you like a gravedigger's Latin.
   Well, I've been childless in the flesh
these fifty semesters,
   but have fathered rich earth
in you, my bean-pole brood,
   my classroom seedlings.
Died without issue?
   "Raise up many disciples"
the Talmud says,
   and if smart-asses count,
I've done that—watched you walk
   white-coated
into the blighted world
   with tricks I taught you,
words I thought wise—
   and how to tell Kernig's
From Brudzinski's sign.
   Died without issue?
My God, I've propagated
   like an over-ripe seed-pod
torn apart—and sent the world
   a thousand children
armed with reflex hammers
   and soldier's heart.

KENNEBUNK POND
In memorium

    She heard
the quivered keening
    of the loons
and shed her clothing
    by the dock.
Shimmering in her flesh,
    she spread herself
on the moon-stippled pond
    and swam out
beyond the barrier rocks,
    ravished
by the lust
    of bullfrogs
and the groans
    of summer boats, hot
to slip their moorings.
    She tossed
one upward glance
    to the sidereal sky,
and then-
    as if to mime
the plunging loons-
    lunged suddenly,
utterly under:
    sucked whole
into that blue quickening
    of stars.

IN MEMORIAM, ILAN RAMON

Ilan, on the morning
   we lost you
in that bright shattering
   of steel,
I had awakened
   from a dream
of Boston
   in early spring.
The April air
   was sweet
and rank
   with loosening earth;
the lilac buds
   beckoned
like young lovers.
   My wife and I strolled
along the Common
   in a bliss
of birdsong
   and crocus.
Then we woke
   to dead February.
What can we do?
   Our prayers
fail us.
   We drive out
to the grocery
   and buy
the ripest mangoes
   we can find.

* Ilan Ramon perished aboard the space shuttle, Columbia

SQUIRRELS

In a January
   colder than buried bones,
the squirrels in our yard
   are Jews.
Shmuel, the sinewy one
   with the gnawed-off tail,
hangs upside down
   from the gutter,
slips tiny fingers
   through the mesh
of our hanging bird-feeder.
   Eli, the optimist,
spends the morning
   fruitlessly shimmying
up the pole
   of the blue-jay feeder-
finally, he eats
   from bird-spill
on the stippled snow.
   Rivka, her belly big
with nipples,
   invokes God's name
and makes a ten-foot leap
   from the maple branch,
landing in a clatter of claws
   on the metal baffle.
Shamed and awed,
   we say a blessing for the young
and scatter birdseed
   on the crusted ground.

www.ingramcontent.com/pod-product-compliance
Lightning Source LLC
Chambersburg PA
CBHW020916090426
42736CB00008B/663